Vegetables

June Loves

CHELSEA CLUBHOUSE

An Imprint of Chelsea House Publishers

A Haights Cross Communications Company

Philadelphia

Chelsea House Publishers
2080 Cabot Boulevard West, Suite 201
Langhorne, PA 19047-1813

The Chelsea House world wide web address is www.chelseahouse.com

First published in 2005 by
MACMILLAN EDUCATION AUSTRALIA PTY LTD
627 Chapel Street, South Yarra, Australia 3141

Visit our website at www.macmillan.com.au

Associated companies and representatives throughout the world.

Library of Congress Cataloging-in-Publication Data
Loves, June.
    Vegetables / June Loves.
    p. cm. – (Plants)
    Includes index.
    ISBN 0-7910-8264-4
    1. Vegetables – Juvenile literature. I. Title.
    SB324.L68 2005
    635–dc22

                                        2004016338

Edited by Anna Fern
Text and cover design by Christine Deering
Page layout by Christine Deering
Photo research by Legend Images
Illustrations by Melissa Webb

Printed in China

Acknowledgements

The author and the publisher are grateful to the following for permission to reproduce
copyright material:

Cover photograph: Pumpkin plant, courtesy of C. Andrew Henley/AUSCAPE.

C. Andrew Henley/AUSCAPE, pp. 1, 15; Jean-Marc La Roque/AUSCAPE, p. 6; Brand
X Pictures, pp. 3, 8 (all), 9 (left and right), 10 (all), 11 (left and right); The DW Stock
Picture Library, pp. 7, 18, 19, 30; ImageBox, pp. 4, 14; Dennis Sarson/Lochman
Transparencies, p. 23; Len Stewart/Lochman Transparencies, pp. 16 (both), 17 (both);
Photodisc, pp. 9 (centre), 11 (centre), 22, 26, 28, 29; Photolibrary.com, pp. 12, 13
(both); Sarah Saunders, pp. 5, 27.

While every care has been taken to trace and acknowledge copyright, the publisher
tenders their apologies for any accidental infringement where copyright has proved
untraceable. Where the attempt has been unsuccessful, the publisher welcomes
information that would redress the situation.

Contents

Plants

Plants are living things. They grow all over the world, in hot and cold places.

Corn is a vegetable that is grown in many parts of the world.

Vegetables

A vegetable is a small plant, or part of a plant, that we grow for food. The **roots**, **bulbs**, stems, leaves, flowers, **fruits**, or seeds of a plant can be a vegetable.

Growing vegetables is fun.

Where Vegetables Grow

Vegetables are mostly grown on farms. They are picked by hand, or by workers using machinery. Many people grow vegetables in small gardens for their own use.

Workers harvest potatoes to sell at the market.

Many vegetables need a special soil and **climate** to grow well. Some vegetables grow better at certain times of the year. Vegetables are also grown in **greenhouses**.

Some leafy green vegetables grow well in a hot, moist climate.

Kinds of Vegetables

Vegetables come from different parts of plants.

Leaves and Stems

We eat the leaves and stems of vegetables such as spinach, lettuce, and cabbage. We eat the stems of vegetables such as asparagus and celery.

spinach

cabbage

asparagus

Roots and Bulbs

Roots and bulbs store food for the plant. We eat the roots of vegetables such as carrots, potatoes, parsnips, beets, and radishes.

We eat the bulbs of vegetables such as onions and garlic.

beets

carrots

garlic

Flowers

The flowers of vegetables such as cauliflower, broccoli, and artichokes are good to eat.

artichoke

broccoli

cauliflower

Fruits and Seeds

We eat the fruits of vegetables such as pumpkin, bell pepper, zucchini, eggplant, and tomato.

We also eat the seeds of some vegetables, such as peas, corn, and broad beans.

bell pepper

eggplant

peas

11

Bean Plant

The beans that we eat are the seed pods and seeds of the bean plant.

leaves

stems

seed pod containing seeds

This is a
bean plant.

Pumpkin Plant

The fruits are the parts of the pumpkin plant that we eat.

leaf

stem

pumpkin fruit

Pumpkin seeds are inside the pumpkin fruit.

How Vegetables Grow

Most vegetables grow from seeds. A seed contains a tiny plant and a storage of food to help the plant grow.

A seed remains in the soil until it is time for it to grow. The small plant that grows from a seed is called a seedling.

The fruits fall to the ground. The plant dies and the seeds remain in the soil.

The small plant grows, and flowers start to develop.

The flowers grow into fruits, which contain seeds.

New Plants from Tubers

Root-vegetable plants make seeds, but they can also grow new plants from their tubers. When a potato plant dies, the potato tubers remain in the soil. The next year, each tuber can grow into a new plant.

potato tuber

shoot

These potato tubers contain a store of food to help new plants to grow.

Carrots take two years to make new plants. In the first year, carrot plants grow their tubers. In the second year, they use the food stored in their tubers to grow flowers and make seeds for new plants.

Carrot tubers help the carrot plant to make seeds for new plants.

Helpful Insects

To make seeds, vegetable plants need a special dust, called **pollen**, from other plants. The flowers of vegetable plants contain pollen and sweet **nectar**. Insects such as bees, moths, and flies travel from flower to flower to feed on the nectar.

pollen

bee feeding from the flower

Insects visit flowers to feed.

The pollen in the flower sticks to the insect. At the next plant, some of the pollen falls off the insect onto the flower. This is called **pollination**. The flower then grows into a fruit with seeds for next year's plants.

flower

small fruit starts to grow

Seeds grow inside the fruit.

Growing Vegetables

Growing your own vegetables is a lot of fun. You can plant the seeds of vegetables such as lettuces, carrots, and beans. You need to dig the soil with a spade before you plant your seeds.

You can pick your own vegetables to eat.

Vegetables, like other plants, need soil, water, and light to grow. A little plant food helps your vegetables to grow well. A layer of **mulch** protects the soil and keeps it damp.

A layer of mulch helps keep vegetable plants healthy.

Grow an Egghead

Plant mustard seeds in an egghead and watch them grow.

What you need:

- mustard seeds
- empty eggshell saved from a boiled egg
- cotton balls
- felt-tipped pen
- water

What to do:

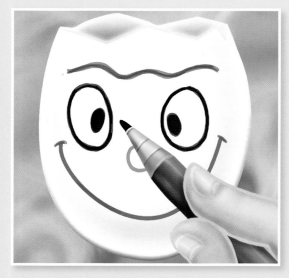

1 Draw a happy face on the empty eggshell.

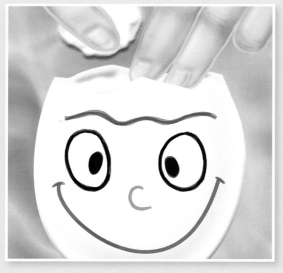

2 Line the empty eggshell with cotton balls.

3 Sprinkle plenty of seeds onto the cotton balls. Sprinkle with water and keep damp.

4 When they grow, trim the plants with scissors.

Tips for Gardeners

Planting vegetable seeds in pots gives them a better chance of growing.

- Small containers or pots are excellent for planting seeds.

- Keep the pots in the light, on a warm windowsill.

- Remember to water your plants!

Plants grown in pots can be placed in a light and protected area.

- Check the roots of your plants when they have grown. If they look tangled, move your plant to a bigger pot or plant it in the garden.

- Always wash your hands when you have finished handling soil.

Scrub the soil from under your nails when you have finished gardening.

Useful Vegetables

Vegetables are important food for people all over the world. Vegetables can be eaten raw or cooked. They can be dried, frozen, bottled, and canned. They can be made into juice, sauces, and pickles.

Vegetable growers send their fresh vegetables to be sold through markets.

Vegetables are rich in **vitamins**, **minerals**, and **fiber**, which our bodies need to stay healthy. Some vegetables, such as potatoes and carrots, are high in energy.

We need to eat many vegetables to stay healthy.

Amazing Vegetables

The largest vegetables in the world are pumpkins and squashes. One squash had a recorded weight of 900 pounds (409 kilograms). A massive pumpkin had a recorded weight of 1,337 pounds (607 kilograms)!

Pumpkins can grow to be enormous!

Glossary

bulb   an underground stem that stores food and water for a plant

climate   the usual weather in a place

fiber   bulky parts of plants that our bodies need to stay healthy

fruit   part of a flowering plant that contains seeds

greenhouse   warm building in which plants are grown

minerals   substances found in food which our bodies need to stay healthy

mulch   a layer of chopped-up leaves or other plant material to help stop the soil from drying out and stop weeds from growing

nectar   sweet liquid made by flowers which attracts animals and insects

pollen   fine yellow dust made in the center of a flower

pollination   movement of pollen from one flower to another

root   part of a plant that grows down into the soil and takes in water and nutrients

shoot   young branch or stem of a plant

tuber   underground part of a plant that stores food for the plant

vitamin   substances found in food which our bodies need to stay healthy

Index